Big Cat Babies

Written and photographed by Jonathan and Angela Scott

Contents

Collins

D0319432

913 000 00126481

Big Cats

In Africa there are wild places
where the big cats live.

Africa's big cats are lions, cheetahs and leopards – and all three are very different.

Their babies are different, too.

Lions

Lions live in a group called a pride.
Their babies are called cubs.

A female lion is called a lioness.
She keeps her cubs hidden until they can walk.

Lion cubs like to play, just like kittens.

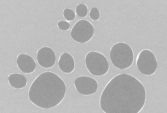

The lioness takes her cubs to meet the rest of the pride.

Cubs learn to live with the pride.

Everyone helps to bring up the cubs.

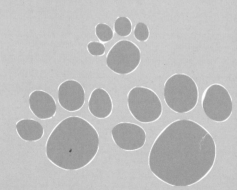

9

Leopards

Leopards live on their own.
They often live in woods where they can hide.

They like to go out at night, just like your cat.

The mother leopard brings home food for her cubs.

She teaches them to hunt.

Leopard cubs
learn fast.

They often want to do things on their own.

Cheetahs

Cheetahs hunt in the daytime.
They are the fastest animals in the world.

They must eat quickly when they kill.
Other animals could steal their food.

Cheetahs are always on the look-out ...

The mother cheetah hides her cubs in the grass until they can run.

Cheetahs can purr, just like your own cat!

They like playing together and will
share their food.

21

Big Cat Facts

Lions		Lions live in a pride.
Leopards		Leopards live on their own.
Cheetahs		Cheetahs are not as strong as lions and leopards.

Lions help each other to find food.	Lionesses help each other to look after the cubs.
Leopards like to climb trees.	Leopards go out at night.
Cheetahs can run at 110 kph!	Cheetahs like playing together.

Ideas for guided reading

Learning objectives: Predict words from preceding words in sentences and finding words that 'fit'; use the term 'sentence' appropriately; use terms 'fiction' and 'non-fiction', noting differing features, e.g. title, contents page, pictures, labelled diagrams; explain their views to others in a small group, and decide how to report the group's views to the class.

Curriculum links: Geography: Passport to the world; Where in the World is Barnaby Bear?

High frequency words: called, do, home, just, live, night, their, want, where

Interest words: lions, leopards, cheetahs, Africa, pride, female, cubs, kittens

Word count: 283

Getting started

- Show the children the Big Cat Facts chart on p22-23, but cover 6 of the 9 boxes. Ensure they understand what a fact is, and read the three facts. Explain that this is a non-fiction text which is full of facts about big cat babies.

- Give children their own copies, and read the title and blurb together, modelling phrasing and intonation. Ask what other things they know about big cats. Jonathan Scott is the presenter of the TV programme Big Cat Diaries; if appropriate, ask if any children have seen Big Cat Diaries on television, and what big cat facts they learned from it.

- Ask them to read the contents page. Discuss which section interests them the most. Can we read that part first? Why?

Reading and responding

- Read pp2-3 as a group, focusing on their reading of each sentence. Ask the children to discuss how